Simply Science
SPACE
Discover Science Through Facts and Fun

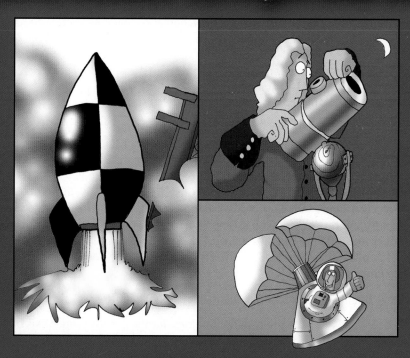

By Steve Way and Gerry Bailey

Science and curriculum consultant:
Debra Voege, M.A., science curriculum resource teacher

 **Gareth Stevens**
Publishing

Please visit our web site at **www.garethstevens.com.**
For a free catalog describing our list of high-quality books, call 1-800-542-2595
or 1-800-387-3178 (Canada). Our fax: 1-877-542-2596

Library of Congress Cataloging-in-Publication Data

Way, Steve.
      Space/by Steve Way.
          p. cm.—(Simply Science)
      Includes bibliographical references and index.
      ISBN-10: 0-8368-9232-1   ISBN-13: 978-0-8368-9232-1 (lib. bdg.)
      1. Outer space—Juvenile literature. 2. Outer space—Exploration—Juvenile literature.
      3. Astronomy—Juvenile literature. I. Title.
  QB500.22.W29   2008
  523.1—dc22   2008012423

This North American edition first published in 2009 by
Gareth Stevens Publishing
A Weekly Reader® Company
1 Reader's Digest Road
Pleasantville, NY 10570-7000 USA

Gareth Stevens Senior Managing Editor: Lisa M. Herrington
Gareth Stevens Creative Director: Lisa Donovan
Gareth Stevens Designer: Keith Plechaty
Gareth Stevens Associate Editor: Amanda Hudson
Special thanks to Mark Sachner

Photo Credits: Cover (tc) Soundsnaps/Shutterstock Inc., (bl) Roman Milert/Shutterstock Inc.; p. 5 Keren
Su/Corbis; p. 10 The British Library, all rights reserved; p. 12 (t) Gianni Tortolli/Science Photo Library; (b)
West Semitic Research/Dead Sea Scrolls Foundation/ Corbis; p. 13 (l) British Library/AKG-Images, (tr) John
Hedgecoe/TopFoto, (br) Randy Faris/Corbis; p.17 Newton Page/Shutterstock Inc.; p. 18 Bettmann/Corbis;
p. 21 (tl) Soundsnaps/Shutterstock Inc., (bl) R. Gino Santa Maria/Shutterstock Inc., (bc) Lance
Bellers/Shutterstock Inc., (br) Pure Digital 2006; pp. 22–23 Telepix/Alamy.; p. 24 Roman
Milert/Shutterstock; p. 25 Chris Cheadle/Stone/Getty Images; p. 26 Alejandro Bolivar/EPA/Corbis; p. 27
Skyscan/ Science Photo Library.

Illustrations: Steve Boulter and Xact Studio, Diagrams: Ralph Pitchford

Printed in the United States of America

1 2 3 4 5 6 7 8 9 10 09 08

CONTENTS

So What Is Space?

Space is filled with visible and invisible forms of energy. In many parts of space, there are rocks of different sizes. You can also find plenty of dust. Space is filled with huge masses of gas—and masses that seem more solid.

We know space has...

galaxies...

stars...

planets...

moons and meteors ...

and lots of pieces of machinery that we've sent up there!

But there's still so much we have to learn about it.

Our Address

We all live in the universe...
in a galaxy called the Milky Way...
in our solar system...
on a planet...
called Earth.

Where Does Space Begin?

You may think that space begins at the edge of the **atmosphere** around our planet. But space doesn't really have an edge. Outer space begins as our atmosphere gets thinner and thinner away from Earth. But where you are now is part of space!

Looking into Space

We know what is out in space because of powerful space telescopes. They are positioned outside Earth's atmosphere.

Any light that comes from a star or planet, or even our Moon, has to pass through Earth's atmosphere. The atmosphere always bends the light, so pictures from telescopes located on Earth may be slightly blurred. Pictures from space telescopes are much clearer.

A Telescope in Orbit

1. The first telescopes used glass lenses to make faraway objects look bigger. But the images were fuzzy.

2. A scientist named Isaac Newton wanted a clearer image. He thought he needed a different kind of **lens**. He wondered if he could use a mirror to **concentrate** the light inside the telescope.

3. He used mirrors to reflect light, instead of lenses to bend it. This helped, but the images were still fuzzy.

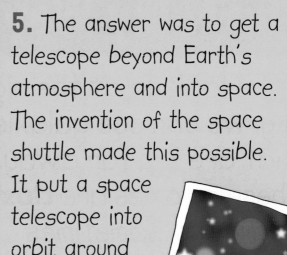

4. Over the centuries, astronomers made more improvements and built bigger and better telescopes. But this still didn't solve the problem.

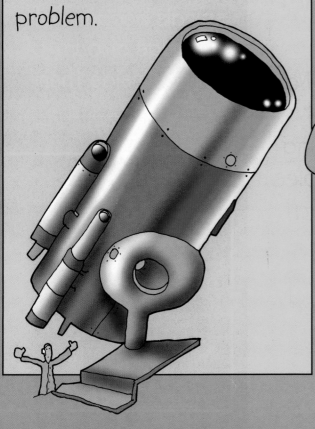

5. The answer was to get a telescope beyond Earth's atmosphere and into space. The invention of the space shuttle made this possible. It put a space telescope into orbit around Earth. At last astronomers could look at clearer pictures!

The Milky Way

If we look up at the night sky, we can see galaxies that are far, far away. These galaxies are **clusters** of millions, sometimes billions, of stars.

We live in a galaxy called the Milky Way. Like all galaxies, the Milky Way is made up of stars, like our Sun. The only reason all the other suns don't seem to look like our Sun is that they are so far away.

Like most galaxies, the Milky Way has a bulge in the middle that may contain something amazing called a **black hole**. Black holes seem to suck in everything that comes near them, even light. Don't worry, though. We're a very long way from the center of our galaxy!

Spirals

Several spiral arms, made up of millions of stars, twirl out from the center of the Milky Way. Our Sun is one of a few stars set apart from these starry spirals. This is lucky, because living things in our solar system would not survive in the main spirals because of the huge amount of energy inside them!

Around the Milky Way

Like all the stars in the Milky Way, the Sun orbits around the middle of the galaxy. It takes an incredible 225 million years to go around once— so it will be a long time before we're there again!

At the center of the Milky Way, there are more stars than in all of the rest of the sky.

9

Our Solar System

A group of planets, moons, **comets**, and asteroids travel on circular paths, or orbits, around our Sun. As a group, these bodies are known as our solar system. The four planets closest to the Sun—Jupiter, Saturn, Uranus, and Neptune—are made mostly of gas.

Asteroid Belt The Asteroid Belt is made up of dust and large rocks (asteroids) that may once have been part of a planet.

Mars Mars is a lot smaller than Earth and only has a very thin, dry atmosphere. It is often called the "Red Planet" because red rocks and dust cover Mars.

The planets orbit around the Sun, held in their orbit by the invisible force of gravity. Gravity is a force that attracts objects to each other.

Earth Home! Here, our atmosphere has allowed life to develop.

Venus Venus is very close to the size of Earth. Its deadly acid atmosphere is 90 times thicker than ours. We could not live there!

Sun

Mercury Mercury is the closest planet to the Sun. It does not have any air or water. Mercury is a tiny, dry, and rocky planet.

Jupiter

Jupiter is by far the largest planet in the solar system. It's more than 300 times heavier than Earth, even though it's made of gas!

Uranus

Uranus is tilted over sideways so much that there are either very long summers or very long winters at its poles.

Neptune

Like Uranus, Neptune is sometimes called an "ice giant" because it contains lots of ice as well as gas.

Saturn

Saturn is the second biggest planet in our solar system. It is famous for the rings that spin around it. Its rings are made of rocks, ice, and dust.

The Kuiper Belt

The Kuiper Belt is a very wide ring around the edge of the solar system. It is mainly made of ice particles. Some of these are huge.

Until recently, Pluto was **classified** as a planet. Now it is thought to belong to the Kuiper Belt. Sometimes its unusual orbit takes it closer to the Sun than Neptune.

The Earth

When the first astronauts rocketed into space, they saw our entire planet for the first time. They saw the blue of the oceans, the greens and browns of the land, and the wisps of white clouds floating above. It was an amazing sight.

Today, hundreds of artificial satellites orbit Earth, sending back pictures just like the one on the opposite page.

Water World

Earth is the third planet from the Sun and the only planet on which life as we know it exists. Most of the surface is covered by water.

The Pacific is the largest ocean. Other large oceans include the Indian Ocean and the Atlantic Ocean. There are huge inland bodies of water as well, such as the Great Lakes in North America and the Black Sea between Europe and Asia.

The continent of Australia is a huge island surrounded by water. At the north and south poles, water is frozen into white ice caps.

The LRV

LRV stands for Lunar Roving Vehicle. Astronauts used these special cars to explore the surface of the Moon.

The Moon is Earth's natural satellite. It is the only other body in space that humans have walked on. The Moon orbits Earth every 27 days, 7 hours, and 43 minutes.

Some scientists believe the Moon is a piece of Earth that broke off after Earth was hit by a huge meteor. Others think it began as a ring of dust around Earth.

A Car on the Moon

1. When the astronauts walked on the Moon, they didn't really walk so much as bounce. That's because the Moon has less gravity than Earth to hold things down. This made moving around very tiring.

2. Despite lower gravity, their spacesuits were hard to move in. They couldn't walk far on their own.

3. They wanted to explore the Moon and needed a way to travel safely and comfortably. So they brought a special vehicle that did not need oxygen to help fuel its engine and which also had tough wheels without rubber tires. It was a lightweight, electric battery-powered "buggy" with wire wheels. They were strong enough not to fall apart on the bumpy surface of the Moon.

4. They called the buggy a Lunar Roving Vehicle, or LRV. It was just right for the job!

Our Sun

Our Sun is a type of star. It is like the other stars we see in the night sky. The only reason it looks so much bigger is that our Sun is so close to us—although you can't really call 92 million miles (148 million kilometers) away that close! We see other stars as pinpricks of light because they are such a huge distance from us.

Stars vary in size. Some are far bigger than our Sun, although most are a little smaller. Stars are made up of gases, mainly hydrogen and helium. The stars are so big and hot that their particles of hydrogen are always moving, smashing into each other and forming explosions that give off a huge amount of energy. We see this energy as the sunlight that brightens up the day and helps plants grow.

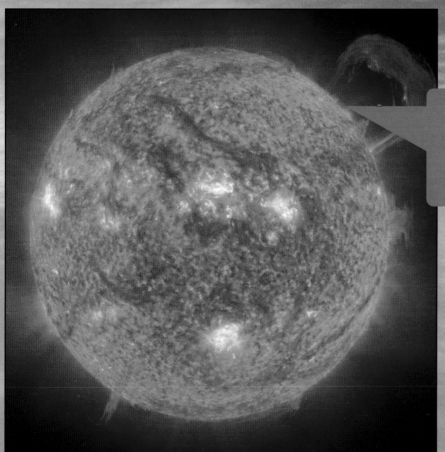

Our Sun is more than one million times bigger than Earth!

WARNING

It's important to remember that it can be harmful to look directly at the Sun. And it's especially dangerous to look at it through binoculars.

The Shuttle

A space shuttle is a spacecraft that can be used more than once.

A space shuttle can be launched just like a three-stage rocket. But it is also able to land on a runway like a plane.

We need to recycle!

A Recyclable Spacecraft

1. Scientists found that sending three-stage rockets into space with capsules on top of them was expensive.

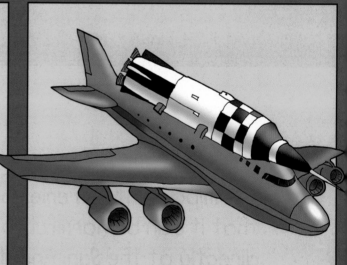

2. They needed a way to use the spacecraft more than once.

3. They had to find a new way of carrying a craft into space along with the tons of fuel that filled its giant fuel tank.

The Orbiter

The orbiter is the winged part of a space shuttle. It sits on top of a huge fuel tank. It gets even more power from booster rockets strapped to the sides of the tank. The orbiter has small engines to help it move around in space.

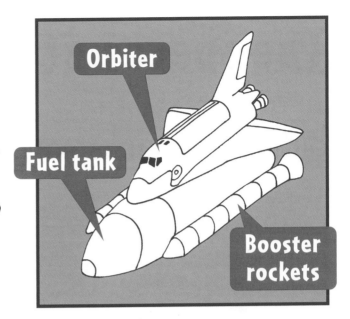

Orbiter

Fuel tank

Booster rockets

4. The reusable craft had to have wings so it could glide back onto a runway on Earth. It needed a heat shield strong enough to withstand the terrific heat created when the craft re-entered Earth's atmosphere.

5. U.S. scientists developed a craft that had its fuel tanks on the outside and was shaped like a plane with wings.

6. They called it the space shuttle. **Ceramic** tiles protected its passengers from the re-entry heat before it landed.

The Spacesuit

A spacesuit is a two-layer outfit worn by astronauts.

The outer suit is a covering that protects astronauts from space particles and radiation. The undersuit keeps them warm or cool.

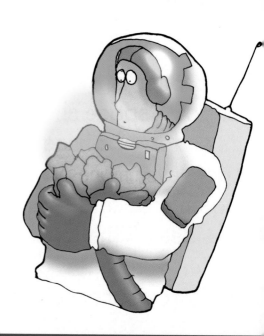

Designing a Spacesuit

1. Although there is no weather in space, it can get very cold or very hot. Astronauts needed a protective suit that could keep them warm or cool.

2. They also needed a helmet to give them protection from the bright light and harmful rays of the Sun.

Breathing in Space

There is no oxygen to breathe in outer space. Astronauts carry a backpack that provides oxygen and removes harmful carbon dioxide and moisture from the air. A spacesuit can keep an astronaut alive in space for up to eight hours.

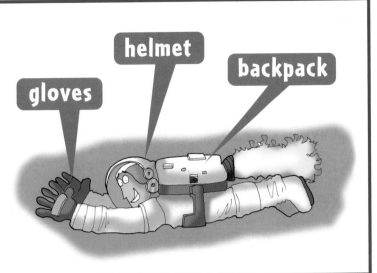

gloves

helmet

backpack

3. Jet pilots already had special clothing for high flying. It kept them warm, but it wasn't good enough for space travel.

4. A space suit also had to protect against space particles.

5. So scientists developed a two-piece suit that would have heating and cooling systems and also protect against space particles and the Sun.

The Rocket

A rocket is a machine powered by gases that explode. Chemicals are mixed with oxygen to make the gases.

When the gas is heated up, it expands very quickly. This causes a strong force that pushes the rocket upward and forward.

The first rocket was invented by the Chinese nearly one thousand years ago.

3. Early rockets didn't go very high. They were too large and heavy. So when the United States wanted to put people on the Moon, they needed something new.

Burning gas pushes out in all directions. Some of it shoots out of the back. This helps push the rocket forward.

A Rocket That Rides Piggyback

1. Scientists in many countries had tried to develop a powerful rocket to go into space.

2. The German V2 was developed during World War II. After the war, many German scientists went to the United States to continue their work with rockets.

4. Then a Russian scientist suggested that a rocket made of more than one section might work better.

5. He was right. The U.S. built multi-stage rockets. Each stage carried its own fuel and engine. When the fuel was gone, each stage fell away. This made the rocket lighter and faster.

A Tiny Space Cabin

1. In space, there is no oxygen to breathe. The farther from Earth you are, the colder it gets. It was hard to make space travel safe and comfortable.

2. One idea was to build a cockpit on the last stage of the rocket. But it would have been a tight fit!

3. Another idea was to put a cabin on top of the last stage. Parachutes could then be used to slow it down when it finally returned to Earth.

4. But the heat and speed that the craft meets when it re-enters Earth's atmosphere would still be dangerous to the crew. And the final bump! These factors were deadly.

5. So scientists built a cone-shaped capsule with a well-protected cabin inside. The capsule was designed to break away from the third stage of the rocket, then parachute down to Earth at the end of the long flight home.

The Capsule

A space capsule is a tiny cabin kept at a certain **air pressure**. It is perched on top of a multi-stage rocket. Astronauts, **cosmonauts**, and space animals have all traveled in capsules.

When the rocket has reached the right height and speed, the capsule is released. It then orbits Earth or takes its crew to their destination.

Once the flight has ended, the capsule plunges back into Earth's atmosphere. A special shield protects the crew from the terrible heat. Finally, the capsule parachutes down to land safely in the ocean or on dry land.

Finding Out

When scientists explore space, there are lots of things they want to find out. What kinds of stars are there? Where do planets come from? Are there things out there we can't see? Is there life in any form on another planet?

Life on the Moon?

For many years, scientists wondered if there might be life on our Moon. But when astronauts visited the Moon, they proved that nothing lives there—not even the tiniest **organism**!

Probing Space

A space probe is a spacecraft with no one aboard. It carries out missions to find out about other planets and moons in our solar system. Sometimes probes go even farther into deep space to send back information. They may one day explore the mysterious black holes and the huge clouds of gas known as nebulae.

Mariner

The Mariner probes sent back lots of pictures and **data** about Mars. But scientists were disappointed to find that there was no life there—just lots of rocks. But they did find out that Mars might have had an atmosphere like Earth's long ago.

Voyager

In the summer of 1977, two rockets containing twin spacecraft blasted off for Jupiter and Saturn. The trip was supposed to last five years, but *Voyager 1* and *Voyager 2* have kept going and going and going!

The *Voyager* probes have sent back many amazing pictures, including this image of a storm on Neptune and its largest moon, Triton.

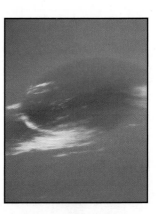

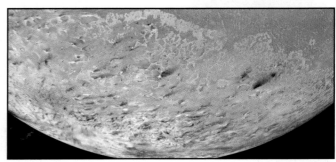

Satellites

An artificial satellite is a spacecraft that is launched into orbit around Earth.

It is programmed to send photos and other information back to Earth.

A Satellite That Gathers Information

1. For many years, scientists wanted to put a satellite into orbit around Earth. It could provide information about our planet and the other planets and stars in space. But how were they going to get the satellite up there?

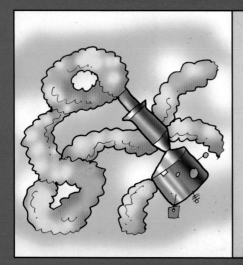

2. A rocket was the only kind of machine that could launch a satellite into space. But it would need to be powerful enough to carry the weight of all the equipment.

Sputnik 1

The first artificial satellite went into orbit around Earth on October 4, 1957. Sputnik 1 orbited Earth every 96 minutes. It was the first human-made object to be put into space. Thousands of satellites, doing different jobs, have been launched since then.

3. Russian scientists developed the satellite so that it was a kind of information radio, or transmitter.

4. Scientists also figured out that if you got the satellite up to a height of 580 miles (933 km) above Earth's surface, its speed would keep it there. At this speed, it would be able to resist the pull of gravity and stay in orbit.

Space Quiz

1. What is the Milky Way?

2. What is the biggest planet in the solar system?

3. What is the largest ocean on Earth?

4. Which two gases are stars like the Sun mainly made of?

5. How many layers does a spacesuit have?

6. In which country were rockets first invented one thousand years ago?

7. What was the name of the first human-made satellite?

8. Which probe sent back pictures of Neptune?

9. What helps a capsule slow down as it lands on Earth?

10. What is LRV short for?

Glossary

air pressure: the force caused by the weight of air pushing down on an area of the ground

atmosphere: the gases surrounding a planet or moon

black hole: an area in space that has gravitational pull so strong that not even light can escape it. Many scientists feel that black holes are super-dense collapsed stars.

ceramic: a product that is resistant to heat and made from a nonmetallic mineral, usually through a process involving high temperatures

classified: placed into a group or a category, often for purposes of identification

clusters: groups

comets: objects in space made mostly of frozen gases and bits of rock and ice. A comet may leave a long vapor tail as it approaches the Sun.

concentrate: to focus, as a mirror might focus light into a small spot

cosmonaut: a Russian astronaut

data: information, often scientific or mathematical

lens: a curved object used to focus light

organism: any living thing

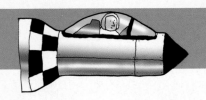